LEARN KARATE

by J. ALLEN QUEEN Fifth Degree Black Belt

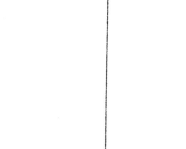

Sterling Publishing Co., Inc. New York

For Tristin and Arielle

ACKNOWLEDGMENTS

I would like to express my sincere appreciation to all of my students who made this book a reality.

Special thanks are extended to Master Larry Bullard and his students for their participation and assistance. Finally, I would like to thank Claire Bazinet, my editor, for her patience, professional assistance, and the personal care she gave to this very special book.

J. Allen Queen

Parents or students desiring information and recommendations about qualified instructors in their geographical area can contact Dr. Queen at: JAQUEEN@MCIONE.COM

Photographs by Samuel Jones III
Edited by Claire Bazinet

Library of Congress Cataloging-in-Publication Data
Queen, J. Allen.
    Learn karate / by J. Allen Queen.
        p.   cm.
    Includes index.
Summary: Introduces the philosophy, uniform, stances, kicks, punches, strikes, and sparring and competition techniques of karate.
    ISBN 0-8069-8136-9 (hardcover)
    1/ Karate for children—Juvenile literature. [1. Karate.] I. Title.
GV1114.32.Q46   1998
796.815'3—dc21   98-26367
                                                                            CIP
                                                                             AC

10 9 8 7 6 5 4 3 2 1

First paperback edition published in 2000 by
Sterling Publishing Company, Inc.
387 Park Avenue South, New York, N.Y. 10016
© 1998 by J. Allen Queen
Distributed in Canada by Sterling Publishing
% Canadian Manda Group, One Atlantic Avenue, Suite 105
Toronto, Ontario, Canada M6K 3E7
Distributed in Great Britain and Europe by Chris Lloyd
463 Ashley Road, Parkstone, Poole, Dorset, BH14 0AX, England
Distributed in Australia by Capricorn Link (Australia) Pty Ltd.
P.O. Box 6651, Baulkham Hills, Business Centre, NSW 2153, Australia

Printed in China
All rights reserved

Sterling ISBN 0-8069-8136-9 Trade
            0-8069-8203-9 Paper

CONTENTS

With this book, you've taken your first step towards learning the ancient art of karate. Congratulations! I'm Dr. Queen, and I will be your sensei (SEN-SAY), or teacher. I have taught thousands of boys and girls how to do karate. Now guess what! It's your turn.

PART ONE

KARATE:
MARTIAL ART
of the MASTERS

Secrets of the Masters

Long ago, the karate masters taught their young students three secrets. The secrets served the students well in karate—and in life.

1 The first secret of the secrets is **Responsibility.**

You must know that you alone are responsible for all of your actions.

In karate, you must be responsible and under control, never striking out or hitting anyone in anger. Acting responsibly in school, at home, and as a member of your community will help you to grow as a person.

2 The second secret of the karate masters is **Respect.**

Always show respect to your karate instructor, teachers, parents, and to yourself. Always do what is right.

Never listen to people who want you to do things that are bad for your body or cause harm to any living thing.

In karate, respect is shown by the bow. At the start of class, students traditionally bow to the sensei. They bow to sparring partners and to judges at competitions. In life, you will soon learn that respect must be earned. You can earn respect by following the directions of responsible authorities, such as your parents and teachers.

rest and sleep. Do your homework and always be your best in school.

Follow the secrets of the karate masters, the three Rs:

3 Rs

Responsibility

Respect

Routine

and you will be on your way to learning karate and improving yourself at home and at school.

The third secret of the karate masters is **Routine**.

A routine is something that you do every day, like having lunch or brushing your teeth, until it becomes a part of you.

Start a daily routine of eating proper foods, practicing karate, and getting enough

ments for exercise, self-defense, and sport. In karate training, you do not actually hit anyone.

One of the first things you learn is control: how to stop your punches and kicks just before contact. You don't want to hurt your practice partners, or anyone. You would only strike a person who is attacking you or is trying to hurt someone else who needs your help—only in self-defense.

What Is Karate?

Karate is an art that began in the Orient over two thousand years ago. It has grown until it is now popular all over the world.

To do karate, you combine leg, arm, and body move-

Why Study Karate?

Karate is one sport that not only builds a stronger body but also gives you a chance to use your physical skills for self-defense.

You can test and improve yourself and enter contests to win awards.

The physical movements you learn are beautiful and fun to do.

You can practice karate by yourself, in the privacy of your own room. Or you can practice with a good friend as a partner/opponent, or with a group— a class in a karate school—all learning the stances, the moves, the kicks, and the strikes together.

Did you know...

The name karate comes from the words: "kara" meaning "empty" and "te" meaning "hand." The way of karate is with empty hands, or without using weapons.

Best of all, while you learn the basic karate techniques or skills and put them into practice, you will find your school grades improving. You will feel better about yourself and gain self-confidence. You will get along better with your friends and your family, and be able to defend yourself if you have to.

It all comes from mastering the three great secrets of the karate masters: responsibility, respect, and routine.

A Difference in Your Life

Karate students soon begin showing a greater sense of responsibility, respect for others, and get into a daily routine of good habits.

As you learn karate, you will become more self-confident and more independent. You will enjoy doing things for yourself and for others. In addition to increased physical skills, you'll find that you are now able to focus. You will

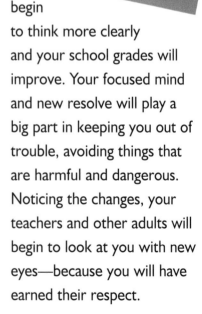

begin to think more clearly and your school grades will improve. Your focused mind and new resolve will play a big part in keeping you out of trouble, avoiding things that are harmful and dangerous. Noticing the changes, your teachers and other adults will begin to look at you with new eyes—because you will have earned their respect.

You'll also be admired by your friends and others your age.

A Time to Learn

What will you learn in this book? You will learn how to do warm-up exercises, then how to punch, kick and strike. You will learn to block an attacker and to spar with an opponent.

Punch

Kick

Block

Strike

You will learn about karate tournaments where you can earn awards and try out your karate skills.

You will learn how to use your body as a weapon for self-defense...

...and learn how to do the most beautiful part of karate, the kata.

Did you know...

Karate tournaments, where you can compete for prizes and test yourself against opponents your own age or at your own level, are held everywhere all year long.

It is always important to show respect to your instructor and to your opponent by bowing.

PART TWO

GETTING STARTED:
A GUIDE *for*
BEGINNERS

Dressing for Action

To train in karate, you must wear either a karate suit or loose clothing, such as a sweatsuit. You need to be able to move freely.

The karate uniform, called a gi (GEE), can be found in some sporting goods stores or ordered from advertisers in karate magazines. The pants usually have either an elastic waistband or drawstrings.

You put on a karate jacket the usual way (1), by pushing your arms through the

jacket's long sleeves (2)…*but there's more!*

With one hand, reach to the other side to find a string. Do the same to the other side (3). You have found the *front* strings, but there are also strings by each side towards the back—the *back* strings.

Take the right front string in your hand and tie it to the left back string, like you do when you tie your shoes (4).

Grasp the left front string and tie it to the right back string (5).

Pull down the sides of your gi to straighten it (6), and you are ready for the belt!

Did you know...

After your first karate belt, usually white for beginners, you have to earn your way up several levels (marked by belts of different colors) before you can wear a black belt.

Belt Tying 101

The belt is very important to the karate student. Its color marks the level of training of its wearer.

As a beginner, you will start with a white or a yellow belt.

As you continue and advance in your karate training, you will earn other color belts—green, red, blue, orange, depending on the karate school you go to—until that wonderfully proud day when you will have the right to tie a black belt around your gi.

First, you must learn to tie your belt properly. You will want to do it right, because a correctly tied belt marks you as a serious karate student.

1

First, to find the middle of the belt, fold it in half in front of you. Hold the two ends together in one hand and the folded "middle" in the other hand (1).

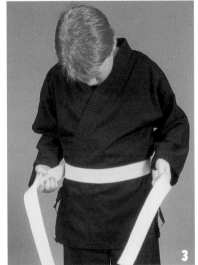

Place the middle of the belt at your waist. Open it out (2). Pass the ends behind you, and to the front again (3).

Pass the left end up between your jacket and belt. Change hands, crossing the belt in front of you (4).

Again, pull the left end up between jacket and belt (5). Pull the ends away from your body. Cross the left end over, then under the right end (6). Knot the belt tightly (7).

Pull both ends and let them fall in front of your gi. (When tied correctly, the belt ends are the same length.) You are ready for practice!

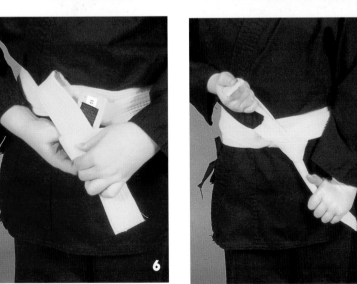

Time to Focus

For karate practice, look for a good-sized area with space to move—like a large room, the cellar, a garage…or outside!

Before you start, you need to focus yourself. You must clear your mind. Get rid of random thoughts and think only of what you are about to learn and do. This quieting process is called meditation.

To meditate, put your knees on the floor and sit back on your heels. Then lower your head and place your hands by your sides, on your thighs, or on the floor in front of you.

Just think of what you are getting ready to do, which is to practice karate. Try not to think of anything else. Usually, you will only need to meditate for two or three minutes. Other times, it may take longer for you to calm and quiet your mind and focus your thoughts on what you want to do.

Before You Start

Always check with your doctor before beginning a program of karate exercises or any other such strenuous program. It's the responsible thing to do!

For safety, buy and use your own mouthpiece…and don't let anyone else use it! When practicing sparring, boys should wear a cup athletic supporter to protect the groin area; girls may want to use a chest protector.

Showing Respect

When your mind is properly focused on your karate training—not everything that has happened to you during the day—get up and bow. This is the way karate students show respect, and it is good practice.

Karate students bow when they enter the classroom at their karate school, and to their sensei, or teacher, and to their partners and opponents prior to sparring.

To do the bow, you need to stand up straight with your feet together and your hands placed at your sides, or a little bit in front.

Bending at the waist, you shift your upper body forward, keeping your back and legs straight.

Sometimes schools have students bow from a kneeling position. The kneeling bow should also be done deliberately and with good posture.

Begin your karate training by bowing at the beginning and at the end of all your karate practices, no matter where you are and even if you are all alone. It is a good routine to get into. Then you will

not have to worry about doing it at other times, and maybe just "forget" to show respect properly...and get embarrassed.

You always bow to your instructor, your practice partner, and to the judges and your opponents in a tournament.

Warming Up

Before you start your karate training, it's important to warm up. You need to do exercises that will get your body ready for practice.

Neck Roll

The first warm-up exercise to do is the neck roll. It is a very relaxing exercise. To do it, you slowly roll your head in a circle.

Stand with your feet a little apart and turn your head to the left (1). Then, roll your head to the back (2)…and, without stopping, on to the right (3). Then finally, straight down in front (4).

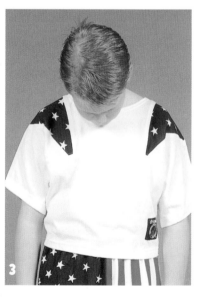

Well, that was easy! You've learned the neck roll and done it once, now repeat the exercise four more times. That makes the warm-up set of five neck rolls.

Arm Rotations

The next warm-ups to do are to loosen your shoulder and arm muscles: arm rotations.

Here, what you do first is just stand up straight, with your feet close together and your right arm down by your side (1).

Swing your right arm forward (2), then upward (3).

Now swing it behind you (4), as if you were winding a gigantic clock.

You finish with your arm back down at your side.

Repeat this arm and shoulder warm-up four more times, and then do the same exercise five times with your left arm.

Finally, make five big circles using both arms, doing two-arm rotations.

Body Twist

To loosen up your arms a little more, and your waist too, now you do side twists.

Facing front, extend your arms out to your sides, like airplane wings, and twist to your left as far as you can. Don't just swing your arms and body, twist deliberately. When you've twisted as far as you can, hold that position (1) for a second.

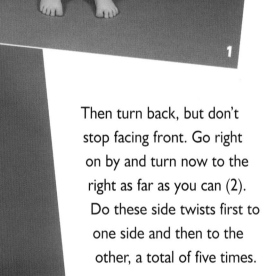

Then turn back, but don't stop facing front. Go right on by and turn now to the right as far as you can (2). Do these side twists first to one side and then to the other, a total of five times.

Leg Stretch

Now you need to stretch your legs to loosen those muscles and make your body more flexible. To do this, sit on the floor or a mat with your right leg folded behind you (1).

Bend forward with both hands reaching out over your knee (2).

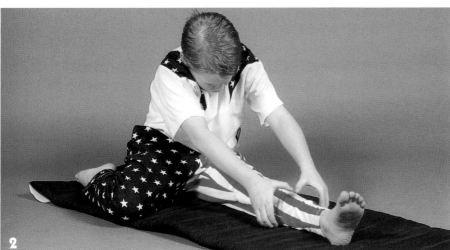

Reach out and try to grab your foot. Hold for a few seconds (3). Stretch out a few more times. Repeat to the other side, your right foot. Be careful not to bounce, just stretch out slowly. Don't bend your knees either.

Toe Hold

Next, you want to stretch your trunk. Sit down on a mat with your feet out forward and together (1).

Stretch forward slowly and try to grab your toes (2). Stretch as far as possible: at first, you may only be able to reach your ankles. *Don't bounce!* Do the toe hold stretch three times.

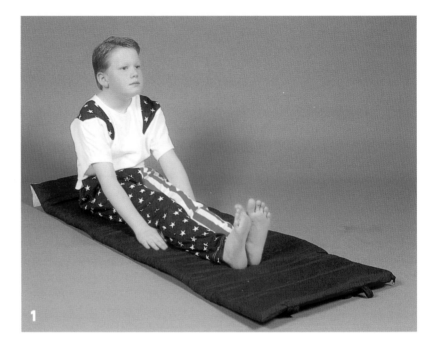

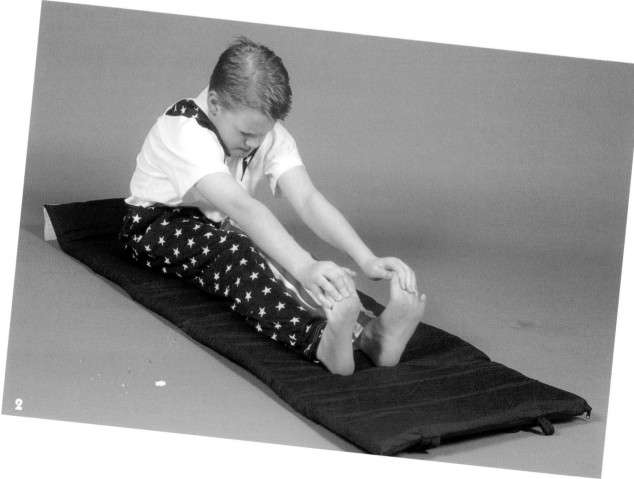

Cobra

Lie facedown and place your hands up alongside each shoulder (1).

Leaving your legs and lower body flat on the floor, *stretch* your head and shoulders upward (2). Do this three times.

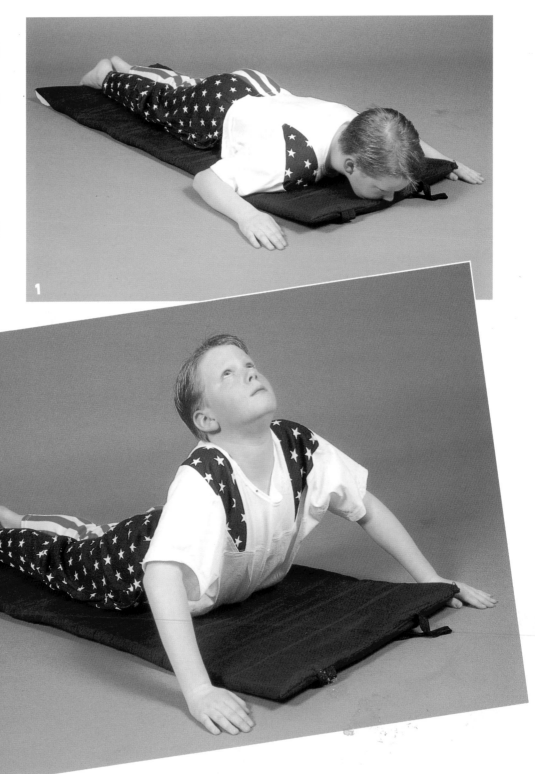

1

2

Leg Lift

Lie flat on your stomach with your arms out in front of you (1).

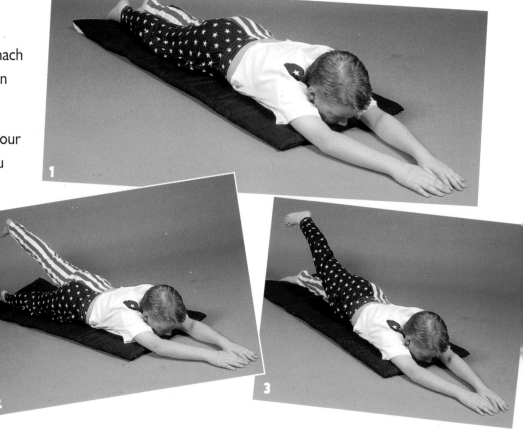

Stretch out and lift your left leg as high as you can (2), then alternate with the right leg (3). Repeat three times.

Butterfly

Sit with your legs in a folded, "butterfly" position (1) and then work your knees up and down…flap them like butterfly wings (2).

Do this for a minute or so (that should be about 30 times).

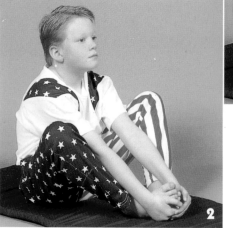

Ankle Grab

Sit on the floor with legs spread out. Reach forward, then to the left over your right leg (1).

Grab your ankle and bend downward over your leg, trying to touch your nose to your knee (2).

Do the same thing with your left leg (3), then switch again.

Repeat the grab on each side for a total of three times.

Deep Body Bend

As you become more flexible you can stretch even farther. Sit down with your legs spread as far as possible and place your hands on your legs (1).

Slowly bend forward and stretch out your hands towards your ankles and bend forward as far as you can (2).

Try to place your head on the floor (3). It's not easy, especially at first, so don't force—and be careful.

Floor Touch

A final group of stretches and you'll be ready for practice. Stand with your feet wide apart and reach way up (1).

Keeping your legs straight, bend down and touch the floor (2). Don't bounce, but stretch slowly. Repeat this stretch five times.

Continue these stretches by bringing your feet *closer* together, as shown below. Stand straight, stretch up, and then bend over and touch the floor. Repeat five times.

Finally, finish the exercise series by putting your feet *right together* like the student at right. Then reach up high in the air with your body stretched up like you did before, and bend down and try to touch your toes or the floor. Repeat five times.

Now you're all warmed up, with your muscles nicely stretched out, and you're ready to learn and practice the basic karate skills.

PART THREE

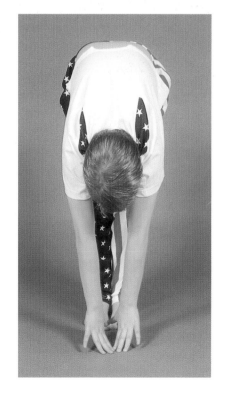

STANCES, STRIKES and BLOCKS: THE BASIC SKILLS

The Stances

A strong stance is the most important part of karate. It is your solid foundation. You are only as strong as your stance. All karate movements begin from a stance. You will learn a few of the basic stances here.

Closed Stance

You use the closed stance, your feet together, to do the traditional bow; your weight is placed equally on both feet.

Ready Stance

The ready stance, with feet shoulder-width apart, is also known as the open stance. You take this stance to wait, and to be ready to move to other stances quickly.

Front Stance

The front stance is one of the strongest and most flexible stances in karate.

To get into this stance, start from the ready or open stance you just learned. Place your right foot in front of your left foot (1) and slide it outward (2).

Bend your right knee and keep a little more than half of your body weight on it.

Lock your back leg; that is, don't bend the knee.

Do the opposite moves to get into a left front stance.

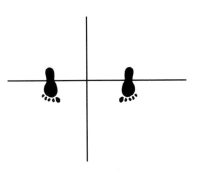

Ready Stance

Front Stance

Back Stance

One of the best stances to defend yourself and to strike is the back stance.

To get into a right back stance start in an open stance—with feet apart. Move to the right by sliding your right foot out to the side (1). Your right foot faces right and your left is in front of you. Set your right foot by placing a little more than half of your weight on the right leg and slide your leg forward (2). Bend the front leg slightly.

Reverse the steps to do a left back stance.

Ready Stance

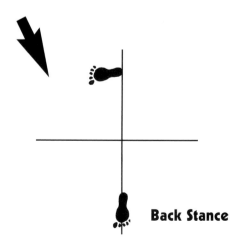

Back Stance

Cat Stance

When you take the cat stance, think of a cat in a crouch, getting ready to strike.

The foot position is almost like the back stance (1), but most of the weight on your back leg.

You set your front leg down lightly, on just the ball of your foot (2). Your front leg is free to strike, and quickly!

Reverse for the other side, placing your opposite leg forward.

Cat Stance

Horse Stance

In the horse stance, you look like you are in the saddle—riding a horse! Your weight is held equally by both legs.

Keep your back straight. Pick up one leg and set it down *firmly* a good distance from the other one. In the stance, keep your feet wide, bend your knees…and stay low.

Horse Stance

Foot Positions of the Basic Stances

Practice going from one stance to another. While waiting for a friend or a bus to arrive, take a foot position. Mentally go through the movements and then do them—slowly and deliberately. Soon, you will be able to switch from one to the other stance quickly and smoothly, without having to stop and think, or make any wasted movement.

Closed Stance

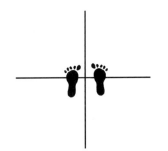

Ready/Open Stance

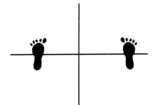

Front Stance
(left)

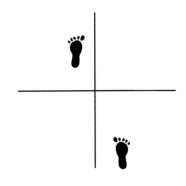

Back Stance
(left)

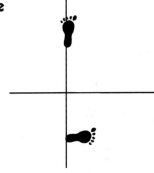

Cat Stance
(right)

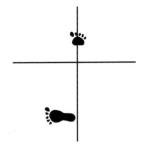

Horse Stance

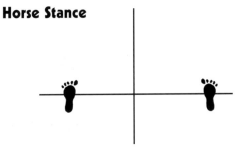

The Kicks

From the stances you can deliver the various kicks, such as the front kick.

Front Kick

In the front kick, you strike with the *ball* of the foot, so you will need to pull your toes back as far as you can.

Start in a *left* front stance (left foot forward) and bring your right leg up with the knee at the highest point (1).

To do the kick, snap your right leg forward, locking your knee as you kick (2).

But then…*snap* the leg back *quickly* to the position just before the kick.

When you do the left front kick, you start from a right front stance. Then you do everything the exact opposite of what you did here.

Side Kick

The side kick is a very strong kick which can be delivered by the left or right leg. The kick must be focused and thrown with a snap from the hip.

To do the kick, take either an open or a horse stance (1) in striking distance of your target.

Pull your left leg up so that your foot is about at your right knee (2), and then…

1

2

…quickly, *snap* the kicking foot out and use the bottom of your foot to strike the target (3).

Important: Just as quickly, you must *snap* the foot back to your right knee (4).

Practice the kick with either leg, and when you can do it well, try for more height.

Roundhouse Kick

The roundhouse kick is a powerful kick to strike a target that is low…

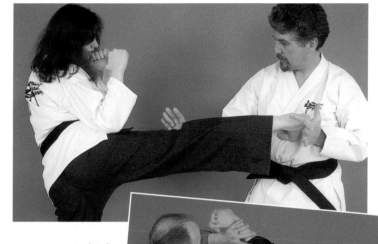

…or high.

Begin from a back or an open stance (1) and raise your left leg behind you with your knee pointing upward (2).

Swing your left leg in front of your left hip and toes, pointing up toward the knees (3).

Continue the circular movement to the right as you kick out with your left leg and foot to strike the target area (4). On contact, retract your kick immediately, going back to the original stance. Do the opposite for the right roundhouse kick.

Did you know...

Your legs are nearly three times as strong as your arms. So your kicks should be three times as strong as your punches!

The Hand Strikes

There's an art to punching karate style. But before you learn the front punch, you need to know how to make a fist.

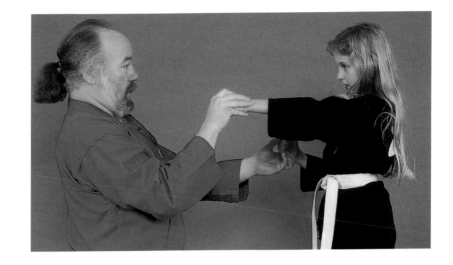

Making a Fist

Let's do it right and learn to make rock-hard fists worthy of a karate student and a karate punch.

This first time, just to learn it well, raise your arms and reach upward, with your hands stretched open (1).

Then, fold your fingertips inward, pressing them against the inside of your knuckles (2), and *roll* your fingers into extremely tight fists (3).

Now you're ready to learn to strike, using a basic karate punch.

Front Punch

The front punch is one of the major techniques, or skills, in karate. It can be used to strike at high, center or low targets (head, stomach, or groin).

To learn, first reach up, with hands stretched wide, high over your head. Make tight fists (1) and lower them to straight out in front of your face (2).

Bring your fists, still tight, down farther in front of you (3). Pull your right hand back, and rest it upside down, palm up, at your side (4). This is the position for practicing front punches.

To start, begin to push the right hand outward (5) and, at the same time, pull the left hand back and inward (6), until it is against your left side.

Finish pushing the right hand out (7) into a punch!

Again, quickly, punch with the left hand and pull the right one back against your side (8).

Now, practice the punches— right, left, and right again. Try counting quietly to yourself: One…

…Two…

…Three! Congratulations! You have learned the karate front punch.

Now it's time to learn some other punches or strikes. All of the punches and strikes can be thrown with either the left or the right hand.

Backfist

The backfist is an excellent technique to use for a quick strike. Prepare your hands (make very tight fists).

To throw a backfist, pull your left fist up to your right ear.

You should be in either the ready stance or the horse stance. For now, keep your right hand by your left side to protect against a kick or hand strike (1).

As you begin the strike, pull your arm forward close to your chest with your palm facing inward. Notice that the right hand returns to the punching position by your right side. This is in case you need to strike quickly with a punch after the backfist (2).

As you snap the hand out fast, keep it on a straight line, right to the target (3).

Strike the target with the back knuckles of the hand (4).

Remember, don't stop! Whip the hand back immediately, recoiling *like a snake!*

Did you know...

In the backfist, it is the recoil that gives much of the power to the strike. The faster the backfist is brought back, the greater the power of the strike.

Palmheel Strike

Another part of the hand can be used in karate as a tool for striking out. The palmheels of the hands are the heavily padded area of your palms, just above the wrist. To hit with the palmheel, you need to pull your fingers back out of the way.

The major target of a palmheel strike is under the chin of an attacker.

In any stance, pull your right hand back to your chest with the palm facing away from you (1).

In one quick move, extend the hand outward...to the target (2). Strike like a snake, by snapping out and returning quickly.

Shuto Strike

Another strike is called the shuto (SHOE-TOE).

This strike is also called the knifehand strike, because the hand is used open and flat—like a knife.

The striking hand is held very stiffly—really rigid—and it is the outside edge of the hand that strikes the target.

Get into a back or open stance and pull your right hand back, your palm facing outward (1). As you get ready to strike, turn your body slightly and then bring the hand around quickly and strike (2).

At the target point, *snap* your hand back to the original position.

Did you know...

The shuto, or knifehand, strike is the correct name for what people who have seen it done in movies have called the "karate chop"— like someone using a chopping knife.

The Blocks

Before you begin putting kicks, punches, and strikes together for use in sparring, you need to know how to defend yourself from those aimed at you! One way is to block the attack.

Upper Block

The upper block is a basic karate block. You use an upper or rising block to stop a downward blow aimed at your head. Get into an open stance with your hands in position as shown (1).

Begin bringing your left arm up and across your chest, palm downward (2). Your right fist is at your right hip.

Turn your left arm so that your palm is facing upward, and *drive* it up to meet the strike (3).

Low Block

Use a low block when you want to block a strike towards the lower areas of your body.

To throw a low block, pull back from a ready stance and place your left arm across your body with your left hand near the right side of the head (1).

Drive your left hand straight downward (2) until...

... your arm is fully extended out in front of you (3).

Outside Middle Block

Next, you need to learn to block strikes to the mid-body. The outside middle block protects from an attacker's middle and high strikes.

From a front or an open stance, push your left hand forward as you pull your right hand back near your head (1).

Begin to turn your body to the right, driving your right arm across your body (2)...

...until it is completely across your front side (3). At the same time, pull your left hand back, ready to punch. Are you getting the idea?

Shuto Block

Like the shuto strike, the side of the hand is held like a knife edge.

Instead of striking downward towards a high target, the side of the knifehand is used to block a kick or punch to the mid-body.

Pull your left hand back with your palm inward, next to your right ear (1).

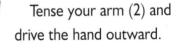

Tense your arm (2) and drive the hand outward.

Complete the block (3).

Now it's time to put all of these skills together so that they form a system of self-defense.

PART FOUR

MASTERING TECHNIQUE: MAKING *the* SKILLS *an* ART

Ready, Set—Combinations!

Are you ready to put the basic karate punches, blocks, strikes, and kicks together into an art form that can also be used for self-defense, as a sport, or just for fun? Try on these combinations.

Practice Your Moves

Get into a left front stance with your left hand in a punch (1).

Step up into a right front stance and punch with the right arm (2).

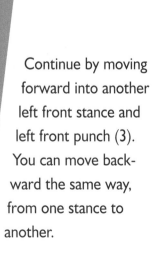

Continue by moving forward into another left front stance and left front punch (3). You can move backward the same way, from one stance to another.

The front punch must have power and good form…

…and the hand must be solidly focused.

Practice kicking hard. First with the right front kick (1)…

… then step down into a right front stance and deliver a *hard* left front kick (2).

More Combination Techniques

Try this pattern. Get into a right front stance (1).

Step forward into a left front stance and do a left downward block (2).

Follow the block by delivering a right front kick (3).

Smoothly, step back into the left front stance and immediately throw a right front punch (4).

Good work! Let's go on now.

Partner Combinations

Find a partner to work with and try some combination techniques. Remember, start every practice with a bow of respect. Then take stances in sparring position, facing each other (1).

Block your partner's punch with a shuto block (2).

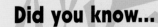

Immediately counter with a left round-house kick to the head (3). (Remember your control!)

Did you know...

To win at sparring you must score three points before your opponent does. You receive a point whenever a kick, punch, or strike at a target area is not blocked.

Step down and finish with a left backfist strike (4).

Block your partner's right roundhouse kick with a center block (1).

Step in and deliver a quick right backfist to the head (2).

Lift your right leg and throw a right side kick to the side of your opponent (3).

Set your right foot down close to your opponent and throw a strong right front punch to his chest (4).

Remember: You *do not* actually make contact! These students and instructors have years of experience and practice under their black belts, and are experts. Use control when you throw your kicks and punches and, in training, learn to stop within one or two inches of target areas.

Face each other and block a
downward strike with an
upward-rising block (1).

Strike with a left front kick (2).

Grab your opponent (3)...

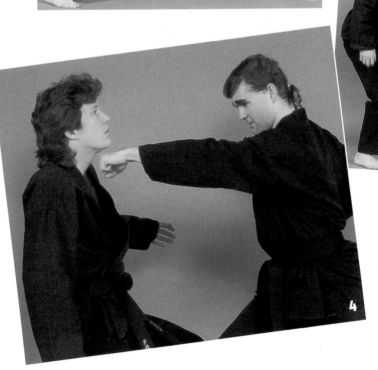

...and deliver a driving front
punch to the head area (4).

Face your opponent (1).

From a horse stance, block a down-ward strike with an upper block (2).

Striking swiftly, counter with a lightning-fast roundhouse to the head area (3).

Sparring (Kumite)

Taking part in tournaments can be fun. If you decide to compete in sparring, you need to wear safety equipment, including headgear and gloves on your hands…*and your feet!*

You would be assigned to compete against someone of your own sex, who is at the same rank and experience level as yourself.

Before a sparring match, known as kumite (KOO-MUH-TAY), each competitor faces the judge and bows (1).

Next, the competitors, who are always of the same rank and experience level, bow to each other (2). Then they get into fighting position.

The judge starts the match (3), which lasts for two minutes or until one fighter scores three points. If neither scores three points, the one with the most points wins. If the score is tied at the end of the two-minute time period, the match continues until another point is scored—for the win.

A fighter earns a point by using a technique that is not blocked. Here, the judge calls for a pause in the action (4).

The judge signals by pointing (5), awarding a point.

If there is no clear strike, or if the strike is blocked, there is no point awarded. The judge signals "no point" by crossing his hands (6).

Practicing Kumite

Now, find a sparring partner and give these a try.

Score quickly with a side kick to the center of the body (1).

This time your opponent misses with a kick (2).

Score, this time, with a backfist to the head (3). You have to be fast.

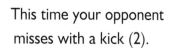

Your opponent throws a front punch, which you block (1).

As you move to score, you are hit with a quick punch to the stomach that scores (2)...

...or with a punch to the head area (3). Be careful! It is not always easy to score. You are on offense and defense at the same time. Learn to use combinations.

In time, and with practice, you'll be good enough at using techniques and combinations and able, now and then, to throw a fake strike that will fool your opponent and score that way. Let's try this one.

Fake a low front kick (1).

When your opponent moves to block the fake, lift the leg higher (2), turning the faked low kick into…

…a high roundhouse kick to the head (3) for the score!

Ready to Spar?

If you can, go to some tournaments and observe at first. Then look for a karate club in your area. Check your phone book or local newspaper. Go and look the clubs over. Ask them if you can just watch, or maybe try one class. Don't be talked into signing any long-term contracts.

Make sure that you get into a class made up of others in your age group and ability… and that the instructor likes to work with kids.

The Kata

A part of karate that schools sometimes overlook, but is the real meaning of karate, is kata (KAH-TAH). Katas are a series of martial art movements, or forms. They are performed at tournaments.

The pre-arranged moves of kata performances look like a dance, but you can use katas to practice the karate techniques that you have learned. Plan out and practice your own kata, using a variety of kicks, punches and blocks. The moves that make up your kata can be changed, so that it becomes more difficult, as you increase in rank.

Did you know...

Popular katas have a name, a number, or both—for example, Heian (HAY-ON) One. Advanced katas look like the movements of animals, such as a cat or tiger or snake.

Katas you would learn in class all have a name or number and are beautiful to watch. But the great karate masters designed them to help their students learn the art of karate. Here is one at beginner level for you to try.

Get into a ready stance (1).

Pull back (2) and deliver…

…a lower left block in a left front stance (3).

Quickly, follow the block with a right front kick (4).

Set your leg down into a right front stance and deliver a left front punch (5).

Turn to your left (6).

Do a left upper block in a left front stance (7).

Do a right punch in the same stance (8).

Throw a left front kick (9).

Follow the kick with a left upper punch (10).

Shift back to the front and throw a lower left block in a left front stance (11).

Close into a ready stance (12).

Remember to bow at the start and the end of all katas.

Good luck and have fun, but remember the karate 3Rs in the first section. In fact, it would be a good idea to review those important 3Rs every day, until they are truly a part of your daily life.

Peace, Love *and* Harmony
to you

INDEX